The Creation

in Full Score

Joseph Haydn

DOVER PUBLICATIONS, INC.
Mineola, New York

Bibliographical Note

This Dover edition, first published in 2001, is a republication of *Die Schöpfung*, originally published by C. F. Peters, Leipzig, n.d. Lists of credits, instrumentation, and contents are newly added.

International Standard Book Number

ISBN-13: 978-0-486-41907-7
ISBN-10: 0-486-41907-X

Manufactured in the United States by RR Donnelley
41907X06   2015
www.doverpublications.com

THE CREATION
Die Schöpfung

Oratorio in three parts
for five solo voices, chorus with SATB soloists,
and orchestra with continuo

Music by
Joseph Haydn

No. XXI:2 in Anthony van Hoboken's *Thematic-Bibliographical Index*.
Words in German and English. German text—based on portions of
John Milton's *Paradise Lost*—by Gottfried, Baron van Swieten,
director of the court library, Vienna.

•

Composed 1796–8

First private performances
Schwarzenberg Palace, Vienna
29-30 April 1798

First public performance
Vienna, 19 March 1799

•

CHARACTERS AND VOICES

THREE ARCHANGELS

Gabriel . . . . Soprano
Uriel . . . . Tenor
Raphael . . . . Bass

Eve [Eva] . . . . Soprano
Adam . . . . Bass

Full Chorus
including SATB soloists

INSTRUMENTATION

3 Trumpets [Tromba]

Timpani

2 Recorders [Flauto à bec]

Flute [Flauto traverso]

2 Oboes

Oboe d'amore

Violins I, II [Violino]

Viola

Bassoon [Fagotto] & Continuo

CONTENTS

To facilitate the quick location of music within this Dover edition,
a section number in brackets accompanies each page number in the score.

PART ONE • *ERSTER THEIL*

PART TWO • *ZWEITER THEIL*

PART THREE • *DRITTER THEIL*

ERSTER THEIL.

1. EINLEITUNG.

Die Vorstellung des Chaos.

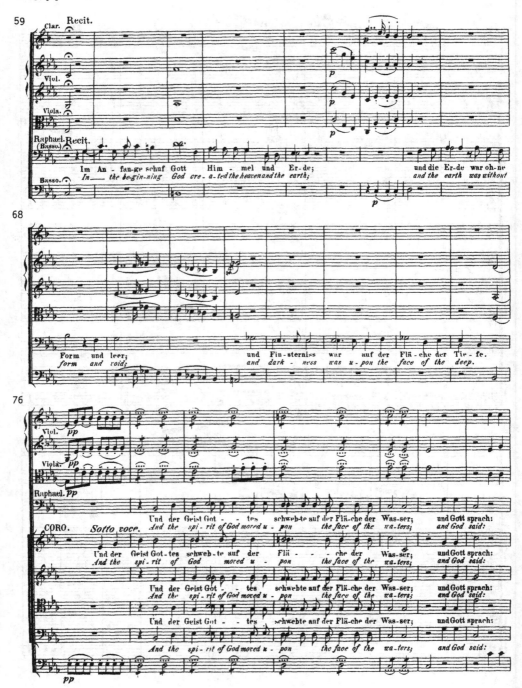

2. ARIE mit CHOR.

Nun schwanden vor dem hei - - li-gen Strahle des schwarzen Dunkels gräuli-che Schatten.
Now va-nish before the ho - - ly beams the gloo - my dismal shades of dark.

Nun schwanden vor dem hei - - li-gen Strahle des schwarzen Dunkels gräuliche Schatten;
Now va-nish before the ho - - ly beams the gloo - my dismal shades of dark.

45

keimt em - por, und Ord - nung keimt em - por.
fair the place, to or - der fair the place.

53

Allegro moderato.

Er-staart ent-flieht der Höl-len-gei - ster Schaar, in des Ab - grunds Tie - fen hin-
Af-frighted fled hell's spi-rits black in throngs, down they sink in the deep of a-

Allegro moderato.

76

83

90

zwei-flung, Wuth   und Schrecken   be-glei-ten ih-ren Sturz.   Und
spai-ring,   rage   de-spai-ring   at-tends their ra-pid fall.   *A*

zweiflung, Wuth und Schrecken   be-glei-ten,   be-glei-ten ih-ren Sturz.   Und
spai-ring, cur-sing rage   de-spai-ring   at-tends their ra-pid fall.   *A*

Ver-zweif-lung, Wuth und Schre-cken be-glei ten ih-ren Sturz.   Und
De-spai-ring. rage de-spai-ring at-tends their ra-pid fall.   *A*

Ver-zweif lung, Wuth undSchrecken   be-glei-ten ih--ren Sturz.   Und
De-spai-ring, rage   de-spai-ring   at-tends their ra-pid fall.

ei-ne neu-e Welt, und ei-ne neu-e Welt ent-springt, ent-springt auf Got - tes Wort.
new cre-a-ted world, a new cre-a-ted world springs up, springs up at God's com - mand.

ei-ne neu-e Welt, und ei-ne neu-e Welt ent-springt, ent-springt auf Got - tes Wort.
new cre-a-ted world, a new cre-a-ted world springs up, springs up at God's com - mand.

ei-ne neu-e Welt, und ei-ne neu-e Welt ent-springt, ent-springt auf Got - tes Wort.
new cre-a-ted world, a new cre-a-ted world springs up, springs up at God's com - mand.

ei-ne neu-e Welt, und ei-ne neu-e Welt ent-springt, ent-springt auf Got - tes Wort.
new cre-a-ted world, a new cre-a-ted world springs up, springs up at God's com - mand.

e - wi - gen Nacht.
end - - less night.

Ver - zweiflung, Wuth und Schrecken be - glei - ten ih - ren Sturz.
De - spai - ring, rage, de - spai - ring at - tends their ra - pid fall.

Ver - zweiflung, Wuth und Schrecken, und Schrecken be - glei - ten ih - ren Sturz.
De - spai - ring, cur - sing rage, de - spai - ring at - tends their ra - pid fall.

Ver - zweiflung, Wuth und Schre - cken be - glei - ten ih - ren Sturz.
De - spai - ring, rage de spai - ring at - tends their ra - pid fall.

Ver - zweiflung, Wuth und Schrecken be - glei - ten ih - - ren Sturz.
De - spai - ring, rage de - spai - ring at - tends their ra - - pid fall.

127

135

143

3. RECITATIV.

Wie Spreu vor dem Win-de, so flo-gen die Wol-ken.
As chaff by the winds are im-pel-led the clouds.

Die Luft durchschnitten feu - ri - ge Bli - tze,
By hea-rens fire the sky is en - fla-med,

und schrecklich rollten die Don-ner um-her.
and aw-full rolled the thunders on high.

Der Fluth entstieg auf sein Ge-heiss der all-er-
Now from the floods in steams as-cend re-ti-ring

33

a 2.

f

f

f

f

p

f

p

f

p

f

qui- cken- de Re - gen,
sho - wers of rain,

der all ver- hee - ren- de
the drea - ry waste - ful

f

38

Violino I.

p

Violino II.

p

Viola.

p

RAPHAEL.

Schauer,
hail,

der leich- te flo- cki- ge Schnee.
the light and fla - - ky snow.

Basso.

attacca

4. CHOR mit SOPRAN SOLO.

15

Tags, das Lob des zwei-ten Tags.
day, and of the se-cond day.

Und laut ertönt aus ih-ren Keh-len   des Schöpfers

And to th'ethe-real vaults re-sound   the praise of

Und laut ertönt aus ih-ren Keh-len   des Schöpfers

And to th'ethe-real vaults re-sound   the praise of

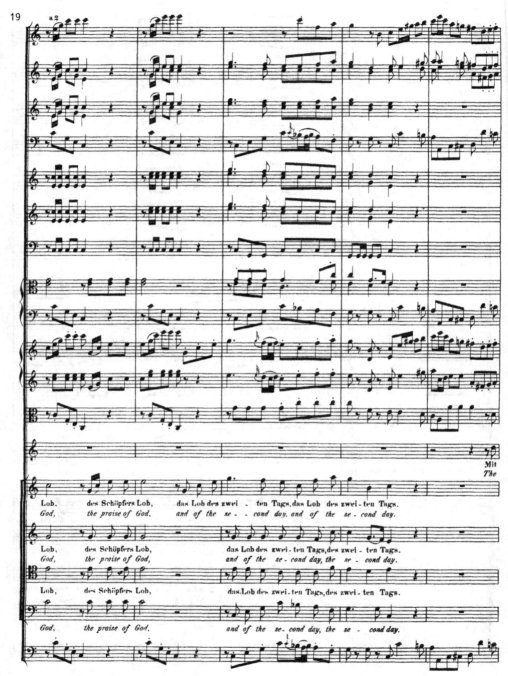

Lob, des Schöpfers Lob, das Lob des zwei - ten Tags, das Lob des zwei - ten Tags.
God, the praise of God, and of the se - - cond day, and of the se - cond day.

Lob, des Schöpfers Lob, das Lob des zwei - ten Tags, des zwei - ten Tags.
God, the praise of God, and of the se - cond day, the se - cond day.

Lob, des Schöpfers Lob, das.Lob des zwei - ten Tags, des zwei - ten Tags.

God, the praise of God, and of the se - cond day, the se - cond day.

24

Staunen sieht das Wunderwerk der Himmels - bür - ger fro - he Schaar.　　und laut_____
marv'lous work be - holds amaz'd the glorious hie - rarchy of heav'n,　　and from th'e - the - real vaults_____

und laut er - tönt des Schöpfers
and from and from th'ethe - real

und laut er - tönt des Schöpfers
and from and from th'ethe - real

28

SOLO.

— er - tönt des Schö - pfers Lob, das Lob des zwei - ten Tags.
re - sound the praise of God, and of the se - cond day.

Mit
The

Lob, das Lob des zwei - ten Tags, das Lob des zwei - ten Tags.

vaults re - sound the praise of God, and of the se - cond day.

Lob, das Lob des zwei - ten Tags, das Lob des zwei - ten Tags.

vaults re - sound the praise of God, and of the se - cond day.

32

Stau - - nen sieht das Wunderwerk der Himmelsbürger fro - - he Schaar, und
mar - - rious work be-holds a-mas'd the glo - - rious hierar-chy of hear'n, and

Und laut er-tönt aus ih-ren Kehlen
And from th'ethereal vaults re - sound

Und laut er-tönt aus ih-ren Kehlen
And from th'ethereal vaults re - sound

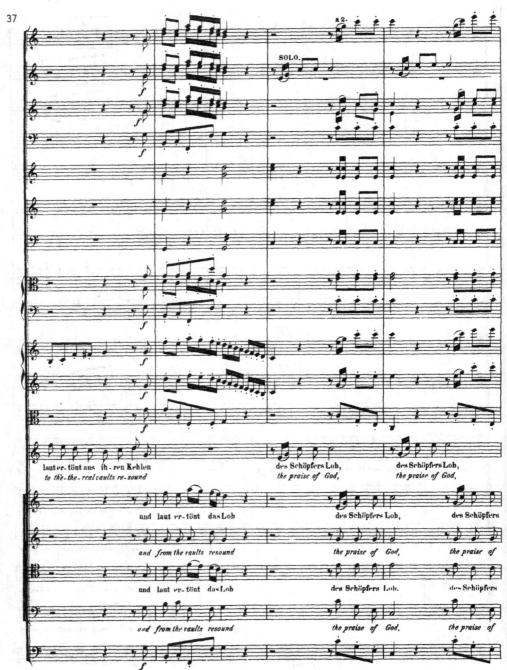

41

das Lob des zwei - ten Tags. Und laut
and of the se - cond day. And from th'ethe-real vaults

Lob, das Lob des zwei - ten Tags, das Lob des zwei-ten Tags. Und laut, und laut' er-tönt des Schöpfers
God, and of the se - cond day, and of the se-cond day. And from the vaults, and from the-the-real

Lob, das Lob des zwei-ten Tags, des zwei-ten Tags. Und laut, und laut er-tönt des Schöpfers
God, and of the se-cond day, the se-cond day. And from the vaults, and from the-the-real

Lob, das Lob des zwei-ten Tags, des zwei-ten Tags. Und laut, und laut er-tönt des Schöpfers

45

— er-tönt des Schö-pfers   Lob, das Lob des zwei-ten   Tags.
— re-sound the praise of   God, and of the se-cond   day.

Lob, das Lob des zwei-ten   Tags, das Lob des zwei-ten   Tags.

raults resound the praise of   God, and of the se-cond day.

Lob, das Lob des zwei-ten   Tags, das Lob des zwei-ten Tags.

raults resound the praise of   God, and of the se-cond day.

5. RECITATIV.

6. ARIE.

Gi - pfel steigt em - por, der Ber - ge Gi - pfel steigt em - por.
to the clouds as - cend, their tops in - to the clouds as - cend.

Hü - gel und Fel - sen er - scheinen, der Ber - ge Gi - pfel steigt em - por, der Ber - ge Gi - pfel steigt em -
Mountains and rocks now e - merge, their tops in - to the clouds as - cend, their tops in - to the clouds as -

por, der Ber - ge Gi - - pfel steigt em - por.
cend, their tops in - to the clouds as - cend.

Die Flä - che, weit ge - dehnt, durchläuft der brei - te Strom in man - cher
Thro' th'o - pen plains out - stretch - ing wide in ser - pent er - ror ri - vers

- der brei - te Strom _____ in mancher Krüm - - - - - me.
er - ror ri - vers flow, _____ ri - vers flow.

Lei - - se rau - - schend glei - - - tet fort, im
Soft - - ly pur - - ling glides on, thro'

7. RECITATIV.

8. ARIE.

9. RECITATIV.

10. CHOR.

4

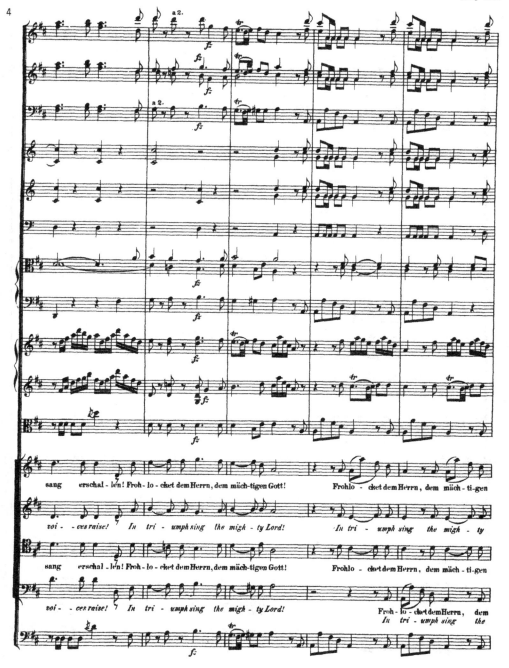

9

18

22

34

stimmt an die Sai-ten,   ergreift die Leyer!   Froh - lo - cket dem Herrn,   dem mäch-ti-gen Gott!
a - wake the harp,   the lyre a-wake!   In tri - umph sing   the migh - ty Lord!

stimmt an die Sai-ten,   ergreift die Leyer!   Froh - lo - cket dem Herrn,   dem mäch-ti-gen Gott!
a - wake the harp,   the lyre a-wake!   In tri - umph sing   the migh - ty Lord!

stimmt an die Sai-ten,   ergreift die Leyer!   Froh - lo - cket dem Herrn,   dem mäch-ti-gen Gott!
a - wake the harp,   the lyre a-wake!   In tri - umph sing   the migh - ty Lord!

stimmt an die Sai-ten,   ergreift die Leyer!   Froh - lo - cket dem Herrn,   dem mäch-ti-gen Gott!
a - wake the harp,   the lyre a-wake!   In tri - umph sing   the migh - ty Lord!

11. RECITATIV.

Uriel.

Und Gott sprach: Es sei'n Lich-ter an der Fe-ste des Himmels, um den
And God said: Let there be lights in the fir-ma-ment of hea-ven, to di-

Cembalo.

Basso.

Tag von der Nacht zu scheiden, und Licht auf der Er - de zu geben, und es sei'n die-se für Zeichen und für
vide the day from the night and to give light up-on the earth, and let them be for signs and for

Zei-ten und für Ta-ge und für Jah-re. Er mach-te die Ster-ne gleichfalls.
sea-sons and for days and for years. He made the stars al-so.

12. RECITATIV.

Flauto I. II.

Oboe I. II.

Fagotto I. II.

Contrafagotto.

Corni in D.

Clarini in D.

Timpani in D. A.

Violino I.

Violino II.

Viola.

Uriel.

Violoncello e Basso.

13. CHOR mit SOLI.

seiner Hände Werk zeigt an das Firma-ment, und seiner Hände Werk zeigt

wonder of his works displays the fir-ma-ment. The wonder of his works dis-

seiner Hände Werk zeigt an das Firma-ment, und seiner Hände Werk zeigt

wonder of his works dis-plays the fir-ma-ment. The wonder of his works dis-

Violonc. e Basso.

44

Werk, und sei-ner Hän-de Werk zeigt an das Fir - ma - ment, und
works, the wonder of his works dis - plays the fir - ma - ment, the

sei-ner Hän-de Werk zeigt an, zeigt an das Fir - ma - ment, und sei - ner Hän-de
wonder of his works dis - plays, dis - plays the fir - ma - ment, the won-der of his

sei-ner Hän-de Werk zeigt an, zeigt an das Fir - ma - ment, und sei-ner Hän-de
wonder of his works dis - plays, dis - plays the fir - ma-ment, the won-der of his

Werk, und sei-ner Hän-de Werk zeigt an das Fir - ma - ment, und
works, the wonder of his works dis - plays the fir - ma - ment, the

60

70

Zun - ge fremd.
un - der - stood.
In al - le Welt er - geht das
In all the lands re - sounds the

Zun - ge fremd.
un - der - stood.
In al - le Welt er - geht das Wort,
In all the lands re - sounds the word,

Zun - ge fremd.
un - der - stood.
In al - le Welt er - geht das Wort,
In all the lands re - sounds the word,

pizz.

89

Più Allegro.

keiner, kei - ner, kei - ner Zun - ge fremd.
ever, ev - er,__ ev - er un - der-stood.

keiner, kei - ner, kei - ner Zun - ge fremd.
ever, ev - er, ev - er un - der - stood.

keiner, kei - ner, kei - ner Zun - ge fremd.
ever, ev - er, ev - er un - der-stood.

Die Him - mel er - zäh - len die Eh - re__
The hea - vens are tel - ling the glo - ry of

Die Him - mel er - zäh - len die Eh - re
The hea - vens are tel - ling the glo - ry of

CORO.

Die Him - mel er - zäh - len die Eh - re__ Got - tes, und
The hea - vens are tel - ling the glo - ry of God,__ the

Die Him - mel er - zäh - len die Eh - re__ Got - tes, und
The hea - vens are tel - ling the glo - ry of God,__ the

99

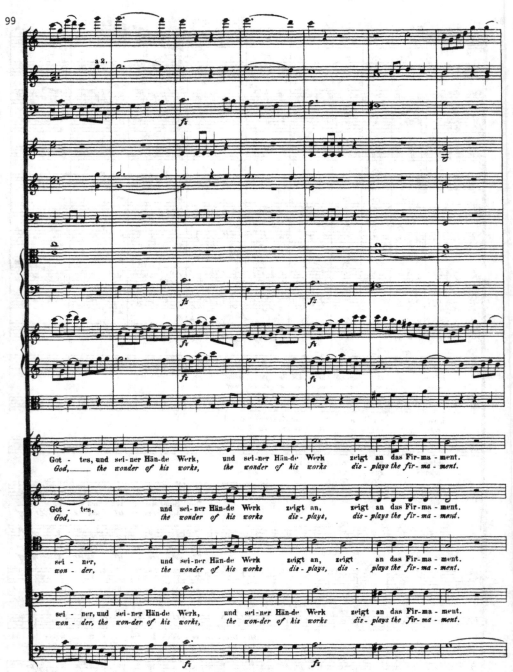

115

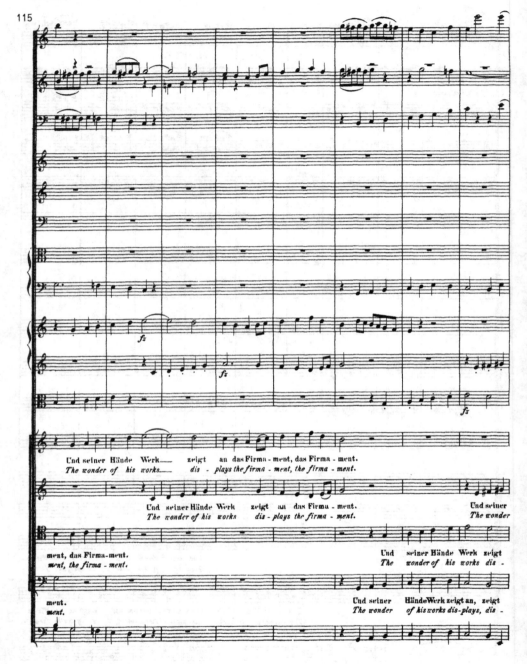

Und seiner Hände Werk___ zeigt an das Firma - ment, das Firma - ment.
The wonder of his works___ dis - plays the firma - ment, the firma - ment.

Und seiner Hände Werk zeigt an das Firma - ment.
The wonder of his works dis - plays the firma - ment.

Und seiner
The wonder

ment, das Firma-ment.
ment, the firma - ment.

Und seiner Hände Werk zeigt
The wonder of his works dis -

ment.
ment.

Und seiner Hände Werk zeigt an, zeigt
The wonder of his works dis-plays, dis -

123

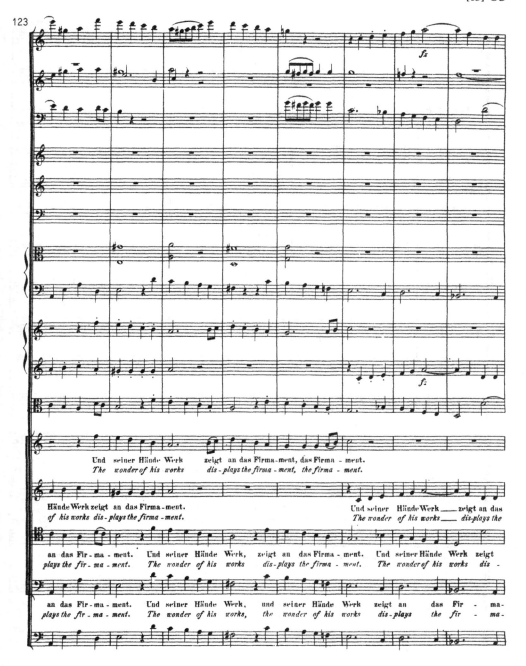

Und seiner Hände Werk zeigt an das Firma-ment, das Firma - ment.
The wonder of his works dis-plays the firma-ment, the firma - ment.

Hände Werk zeigt an das Firma-ment.
of his works dis-plays the firma-ment.

Und seiner Hände Werk____ zeigt an das
The wonder of his works____ dis-plays the

an das Fir - ma - ment. Und seiner Hände Werk, zeigt an das Firma - ment. Und seiner Hände Werk zeigt
plays the fir - ma - ment. The wonder of his works dis-plays the firma - ment. The wonder of his works dis -

an das Fir - ma - ment. Und seiner Hände Werk, und seiner Hände Werk zeigt an das Fir - ma
plays the fir - ma - ment. The wonder of his works, the wonder of his works dis-plays the fir - ma-

131

139

Werk, und sei - ner Hände Werk zeigt an, zeigt an das Fir - ma - ment. Die Himmel er - zäh - len die
works, the won-der of his works dis-plays, dis-plays the fir - ma - ment. The hea-vens are tel - ling the

Werk, und sei-ner Hände Werk zeigt an, zeigt an das Fir ma - ment. Die Himmel er-
works, the won-der of his works dis-plays, dis-plays the fir - ma - ment. The hea-vens are

seiner Hände Werk zeigt an das Fir - ma - ment, das Fir - ma - ment. Die Himmel er - zäh - len die Eh -
wonder of his works dis-plays the fir - ma - ment, the fir - ma - ment. The hea-vens are tel - ling the glo -

Werk, und sei - ner Hände Werk zeigt an, zeigt an das Fir - ma - ment. Die Himmel er - zäh - len die
works, the won-der of his works dis-plays, dis-plays the fir - ma - ment. The hea-vens are tel - ling the

156

Eh - - re Got - tes,und seiner Hände Werk zeigt an das Firma - ment, zeigt an das Firma - ment, zeigt
glo - ry of God, the wonder of his works dis - plays the firma - ment, dis - plays the firma - ment, dis -

zäh - len die Eh - - re Got - tes, und seiner Hände Werk zeigt an das Firma -
tel - ling the glo - - ry of God, the wonder of his works dis - plays the firma -

- - re Got - tes,und seiner Hände Werk zeigt an das Firma - ment, zeigt an das Firma - ment, zeigt
ry of God, the wonder of his works dis - plays the firma - ment, dis - plays the firma - ment, dis -

Eh - re Got - tes,und seiner Hände Werk _____ zeigt an, _____ zeigt an _____
glo - ry of God, the wonder of his works _____ dis - plays, _____ dis - plays, _____

ff

164

an＿＿das Firma - ment. Und seiner Hände Werk zeigt au das Firma - ment, zeigt an, zeigt
plays＿＿the firma - ment. The wonder of his works dis-plays the firma - ment, dis-plays, dis-

ment, das Fir - ma - ment. Und seiner Hände Werk zeigt an das Firma - ment, zeigt an, zeigt
ment. the fir - ma - ment. The wonder of his works dis-plays the firma - ment, dis-plays, dis-

an＿＿das Firma - ment. Und seiner Hände Werk zeigt an das Fir - ma - ment, das
plays＿＿the firma - ment. The wonder of his works dis-plays the fir - ma - ment, the

＿＿das Firma - ment. Und seiner Hände Werk zeigt an das Firma - ment, zeigt an, zeigt
＿＿the firma - ment. The wonder of his works dis-plays the firma - ment, dis-plays, dis-

180

ZWEITER THEIL.
14. RECITATIV.

15. ARIE.

34

Gabriel.

Auf star - - kem Fit - - ti-ge schwinget sich der Ad - ler stolz, der Ad - ler stolz, und
On migh - - ty pens up - lift - ed soars the eagle a - loft, the ea - gle a - loft, and

41

Viol.I.

Viol.II.

Viola.

thei - let die Luft im schnel - le - sten Flu - ge zur Son - ne hin, zur
cleares the sky in swift - est flight, in swift - est flight to the bla - zing sun, to the

47

Fl.

Clar.

Fag.

a 2.

SOLO.

Son - ne hin.
bla - zing sun.

Den Mor - gen grüsst der
His wel - come bids to

Vcello.
unis.

Aus je - dem
From ev' - ry

Busch___ und Hain er-schallt der Nach-ti - gal - len sü - sse Keh - le.
bush___ and grove re - sound the night - in - gale's de - light - ful notes.

Noch drück - te Gram nicht ih-re Brust,
No grief af - fect - ed yet her breast.

noch war zur Kla-ge nicht ge-stimmt ihr reizender, ihr
nor to a mournful tale were tun'd her soft, her

rei-zender Ge-sang, ihr rei - - - - -
soft enchanting lays. her soft

zender, ihr
en-chant-ing, her

reizen-der Ge - sang.
soft en-chanting lays.

Noch drückte Gram nicht ih-re Brust,
No grief af - fect-ed yet her breast,

noch war zur Kla-ge nicht ge-stimmt
nor to a mourn-ful tale were tun'd

ihr reizender,
her soft,___

ihr rei - zender Ge-sang,
her soft___ enchanting lays,

ihr rei - - - - - - - zender Ge-
her soft_____ enchanting

16. RECITATIV.

Mehret euch, ihr Fluthenbe wohner.
Multi ply, ye fin ny tribes.
und fül let je de Tie fe!
and fill each watry drop.
Seid fruchtbar, wachset,
Be fruitful, grow and

(divisi)

meh ret euch!
mul ti ply!
Er freu et euch in eu rem Gott,
And in your God and Lord re joice,
er freu et euch in eu rem Gott!
and in your God and Lord re joice!

17. RECITATIV.

Raphael. Recit.

Und die En gel rühr ten ihr' un sterb li chen
And the an gels struck their im mor tal

Cembalo.

Basso.

Har fen, und san gen die Wunder, und san gen die Wun der des fünf ten Tag's.
harps and the wonders, the won ders of the fifth day sung.

18. TERZETT.

attacca

19. CHOR mit SOLI.

15

22

26

31

40

58

61

20. RECITATIV.

21. RECITATIV.

Das zackge Haupt er-hebt der schnelle Hirsch.
The nimble stag bears up his branching head.

Mit flie-gender Mäh-ne springt und wiehrt voll Muth und Kraft das ed-le Ross
With fly- -ing ma-ne and fie-ry look, im - pa-tient neighs the spright-ly steed.

Auf grü-nen Matten weidet schon das Rind, in
The cattle in herds al - ready seeks his food on

22. ARIE.

Nun scheint in vol - lem Glan - ze der Himmel.
Now heav'n in ful - lest glo - ry shone;

al - - les nicht vollbracht. Dem Ganzen fehl - - te das Ge-schöpf, das Got-tes Wer-ke dank - - bar sehn, des
work was not com-plete. There wanted yet that wondrous be - ing, that grate-ful should God's powr - - ad-mire, with

Her - ren Gü - te prei - sen soll, das Got - tes Werke dank - bar
heart and voice his goodness praise, that grate - ful should God's powr ad -

23. RECITATIV.

24. ARIE.

Mit Würd' und Ho - heit an - ge-than, mit
In na - tive worth and ho-nour clad, with

ver - kündt der Weis - heit tie - fen Sinn, und aus dem hel - len
of wis - dom deep de - clares the seat, and in his eyes with

Bli - cke strahlt der Geist, des Schö - pfers Hauch und E - ben - bild.
bright - ness shines the soul, the breath and i - mage of his God.

ihm Lie - be,   ihm Lie - be,   Glück _ und Won - ne zu,
be - speak _   him love, _   love _ and joy _ and bliss,

ihm Lie-be,   Glück   und Won - - - - - ne zu. _
be-speak him   love   and joy _ _ _ _ _ and bliss. _

25. RECITATIV.

26. CHOR.

6

len - det ist das gro - sse Werk, der Schö - pfer sieht's und freu - et
chie - ved is the glo - rious work, the Lord be - holds it and is

len - det ist das gro - sse Werk, der Schö-pfer sieht's und freu - et sich, und freu - et
chie - ved is the glo - rious work, the Lord be-holds it and is pleas'd, and is

len - det ist das gro - sse Werk, der Schö - pfer sieht's und freu - et
chie - ved is the glo - rious work, the Lord be - holds it and is

len - det ist das gro - sse Werk, der Schö-pfer sieht's und freu - et sich, der Schö - pfer sieht's und freuet
chie - ved is the glo - rious work, the Lord be-holds it and is pleas'd, the Lord be-holds it and is

11

sich,   der Schöpfer sieht's   und freuet   sich.
pleas'd,   the Lord be - holds it   and is   pleas'd.

sich,   der Schöpfer sieht's   und freuet   sich.
pleas'd,   the Lord be - holds it   and is   pleas'd.

sich,   der Schöpfer sieht's   und freuet   sich.   Auch uns-re Freud'   er-
pleas'd,   the Lord be - holds it   and is   pleas'd.   In lof - ty strains   let

sich,   der Schöpfer sieht's   und freuet   sich.   Auch uns-re Freud'   er-schal - le
pleas'd,   the Lord be - holds it   and is   pleas'd.   In lof - ty strains   let us____   re-

27

32

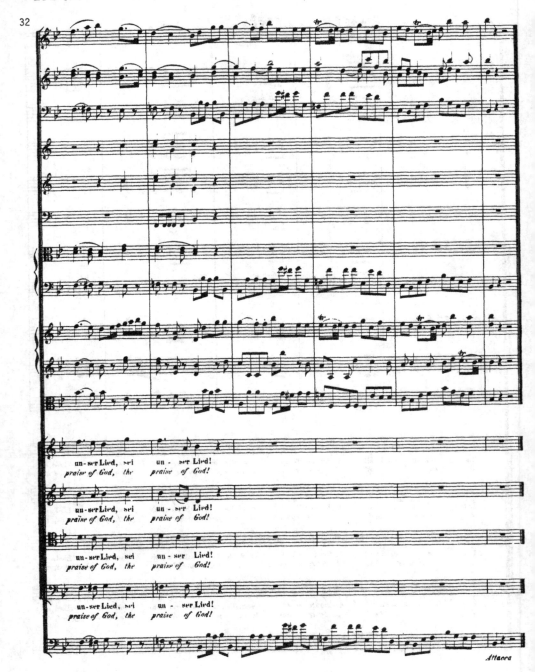

un-ser Lied, sei   un-ser Lied!
praise of God, the   praise of God!

un-ser Lied, sei   un-ser Lied!
praise of God, the   praise of God!

un-ser Lied, sei   un-ser Lied!
praise of God, the   praise of God!

un-ser Lied, sei   un-ser Lied!
praise of God, the   praise of God!

Attacca

27. TERZETT.

82

88

Attacca.

28. CHOR.

30

al - le - lu - ja,
- men, al - le - lu - ja,
- er, al - le - lu - ja.

al - le - lu - ja, al - le - lu - ja.   Al - les lo - be sei - nen Na - - men, al - le - lu -
al - le - lu - ja, al - le - lu - ja.   Glo - ry to his name for er - er, al - le - lu -

ja.   Al - - les lo - be sei - nen Na - - - men, al - le - lu - - ja, al - le - lu -
ja.   Glo - - ry to his name for er - - - er, al - le - lu - ja, al - le - lu -

men.   Al - - les lo - be sei - nen Na - - men.   al - le - lu - ja, al - le - lu -
er.   Glo - - ry to his name for er - - er,   al - le - lu - ja, al - le - lu -

34

43

47

55

59

71

hoch er-ha - ben, ist hocher-ha - ben, al - le - lu - ja, al - le - lu - ja.
alt - - ed reigns, ex-alt-ed reigns, al - le - lu - ja, al - le - lu - ja.

ist hocher-ha - ben, ist hocher-ha - ben, al - le - lu - ja, al - le - lu - ja.
ex-alt-ed reigns, ex-alt-ed reigns, al - le - lu - ja, al - le - lu - ja.

hoch er-ha - ben, ist hocher-ha - ben, al - le - lu - ja, al - le - lu - ja.
alt - - ed reigns, ex-alt-ed reigns, al - le - lu - ja, al - le - lu - ja.

ist hocher-ha - ben. ist hocher-ha - ben. al - le - lu - ja, al - le - lu - ja.
ex-alt-ed reigns, ex-alt-ed reigns, al - le - lu - ja, al - le - lu - ja.

Ende des zweiten Theils.

DRITTER THEIL.

29. RECITATIV.

174

30. DUETT und CHOR.

22

27

37

ü - ber - all sein Lob in eu - rem Chor - ge sang.
ev' - ry where his praise in cho - ral songs__ a - bout!

Adam.

Ihr E - le - men - te,
Ye strong and cum - brous,

de - ren Kraft stets neu - e For - men zeugt, stets neu - e Formen zeugt, ihr,
strong e - le - ments who ceas - less changes make, who ceas - less changes make, ye,

ihr Dünst' und Ne - bel, die der Wind ver - sam - melt und ver - treibt, ver - sam - melt und ver -
ye dus - ky mists and dew - y steams who raise and fall thro' th'air. who raise and fall thro'

143

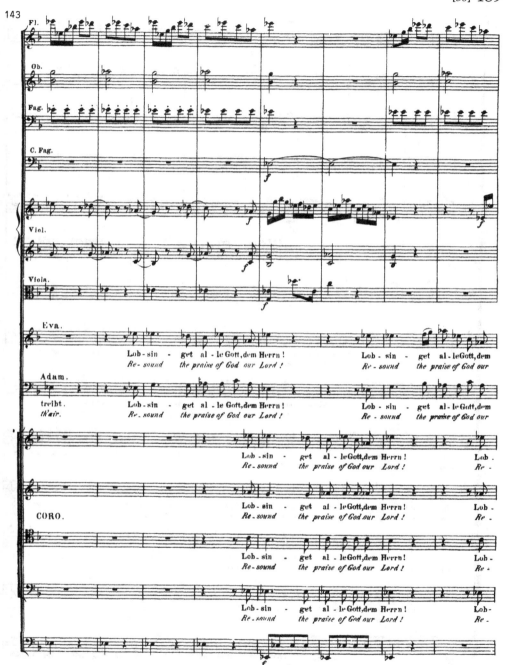

151

263

271

280

Him - mel an; wir preisen dich in E - wig - keit, wir prei-sen dich in
heav'n and earth; we praise thee now and ev - er more, we praise thee now and

Him - mel an; wir preisen dich in E - wig-keit, wir
heav'n and earth; we praise thee now and ev - er more, we

Him - mel an; wir preisen dich in E - wig -
heav'n and earth; we praise thee now and ev - er

Him - mel an; wir preisen dich in E - wig - keit, wir prei-sen dich in
heav'n and earth; we praise thee now and ev - er more, we praise thee now and

317

prei - sen dich in E - wig - keit,   wir prei - sen dich in E - wig - keit,   wir
praise thee now and ev - er more,   we praise thee now and ev - er more,   we

prei - - sen dich, wir prei - sen dich in E - wig - keit,   in E - wig - keit,   wir
praise   thee now,   we praise thee now and ev - er more,   and ev - er more,   we

keit,   wir prei - sen dich in E - - - wig - keit,   wir
more   we praise thee now and ev - - - er more,   we

prei - sen dich in E - wig - keit,   wir prei - sen dich in E - wig - keit,   wir
praise thee now and ev - er more,   we praise thee now and ev - er more,   we

324

prei-sen dich in E - - - - - - wig-keit.

praise thee now and ev - - - - - - - - er more.

prei-sen dich in E - - - - - - - wig-keit.

praise thee now and en - - - - - - - er more.

332

341

prei - - sen dich, wir prei-sen dich in E - wigkeit, in

praise _____ thee now, we praise thee now and ev - er more, and

prei - - sen dich, wir prei-sen dich in E - wigkeit, in

praise _____ thee now, we praise thee now and ev - er more, and

349

369

378

keit, in E - wig - keit.

more, and ev - er more.

keit, in E - wig keit.

more, and ev - er more.

31. RECITATIV.

35

und dir ge - hor - chen bringt mir Freu - - - de, Glück und Ruhm
and from o - be - dience grows my pride_____ and hap - pi - ness.

32. DUETT.

Flauto I. II.

Oboe I. II.

Clarinetto I. II. in B.

Fagotto I. II.

Corni in Es.

Violino I.

Violino II.

Viola.

Eva.

Adam.

Violoncello e Basso.

7

Adagio.

Hol - - de Gat - tin! dir zur Sei - te flie - ssen
Grace - - ful consort! At thy side_____ soft - ly

81

90

Die Kuh-le des A-bends, o wie er-quicket sie!
The coolness of ev'n, o how she all restores!

Fl.

SOLO.

p

Wie rei-zend
How pleasing

Wie la-bend ist der runden Früchte Saft!
How gra-te-ful is of fruits the sa-vour sweet!

der A-bendhauch,
the breath of ev'n,

der Blu-menDuft!
the fragrant bloom!

Morgenthau,
morning dew,

derFrüchteSaft,
the sav'ry fruit,

Mit dir, mit dir er-höht sich je-de Freude;
With thee, with thee is ev'-ry joy en-hanced;

mit dir, mit dir geniess' ich doppelt
with thee, with thee de-light is ev-er

Mit dir, mit dir er-höht sich je-de Freude;
With thee, with thee is ev'-ry joy en-hanced;

mit dir, mit dir geniess' ich doppelt
with thee, with thee de-light is ev-er

33. RECITATIV.

34. SCHLUSSCHOR (mit SOLI.)

Lasst zu Eh - ren sei - nes Namens Lob in Wett-gesang er - schal - - - len.

Ce - le-brate his pow'r and glo-ry. Let his name resound on high! ____

Lasst zu Eh - ren sei - nes Namens Lob in Wett-gesang er - schal - - len.

Ce - le-brate his pow'r and glo-ry. Let his name resound on high! ____

men.
men.

A - - - men.
A - - - men.

bleibt in E - wig-keit.
praise shall last for aye.

A - - - men.
A - - - men.

E wigkeit, in E - wig-keit. A - - - men.
last for aye, shall last for aye. A - - - men.

Des Herren Ruhm, er
The Lord is great, his

Ruhm, er bleibt in E - wigkeit. A - - - men.
great, his praise shall last for aye. A - - - men.

Des Herren
The Lord is

Vcello.

unis.

32

keit. A - - - men. Des Herren Ruhm, er bleibt in E - wigkeit.
aye. A - - - men The Lord is great, his praise shall last for aye.

Ruhm, er bleibt in E - wigkeit. Des Herren Ruhm, er bleibt in E - wigkeit.
great, his praise shall last for aye. The Lord is great, his praise shall last for aye.

- men, a - men, a - - - - - men. Er bleibt in E - wigkeit.
- men, a - men, a - - - - - men. his praise shall last for aye.

- men, a - men, a - men, a - - men. Er bleibt in E - wig-
- men, a - men, a - men, a - - men. his praise shall last for

Veello.

unis.

40

44

48

keit. A - - - - - men. Des Her-ren Ruhm, er bleibt in E - wig-
aye. A - - - - - men. The Lord is great, his praise shall last for

men, a - - - - men.
men, a - - - - men.

keit, in E -wig-keit.
aye, shall last for aye.

Des Her-ren Ruhm, er bleibt in E - wig-
The Lord is great, his praise shall last for

Des Her-ren Ruhm, er bleibt in E - wig-keit. A -
The Lord is great, his praise shall last for aye. A -

unis.

52

56

60

A - - men, a - - men, a - - - -
A - - men, a - - men,

A - men, a - men, a - - - -
A - - men, a - - men, a - - - -

A - men, Des Her ren Ruhm, er bleibt in E - wig-
A - - men, The Lord is great, his praise shall last for

- - men.
- - men.

a - - men.
a - - men.

a - - men.
a - - men.

E - - wigkeit.
last for aye.

Vc.   Vc.
p   punis.   unis.

64

78

Herren   al-le Stimmen!   Des Herren Ruhm, er bleibt in   E - wigkeit. A - men.   A - men.
Lord   ut-ter thanks!   The Lord is great, his praise shall last for aye. A - men.   A - men.

ENDE.